Realisations

Of An Always Searching Mind That Came To Rest

Jonathan Rohrer

Copyright © 2021
All Rights Reserved

Table of Contents

Dedication i
Acknowledgement ii
About The Author iv
Introduction 1
Chapter 1: Balance 6
Chapter 2: About Judgment... 11
Chapeter 3: Growing (Up) 13
Chapter 4: Freedom 19
Chapter 5: Don't Workout Because You Hate Yourself . 25
Chapter 6: People Change 28
Chapter 7: The Outside 32
Chapter 8: There Is No Right Decision 33
Chapter 9: Don't Ever Think You Are Too Broken To Be Fixed 36
Chapter 10: Don't Be Afraid To Ask For Help 40
Chapter 11: Never Forget The Value Of Time 44
Chapter 12: The Truth Is: There Is No Truth 48
Chapter 13: People Hurt People Because They Got Hurt 52
Chapter 14: You Don't Need To Hope 55
Chapter 15: Stop Trying To Fix Things............................ 61
Chapter 16: Be Kind 68
Epilogue.. 72
Books 74
Movies and Series... 75

Dedication

This book was originally dedicated to me, because the notes it is based on were intended for my future self. So I wouldn't forget about these realisations and could meditate on them.

But as I realised that those perspectives can be beneficial to others, I decided to write this book and thereby dedicate to them.

Acknowledgement

I am first of all acknowledging all my friends. People that I met at some point of my life, be it many years ago or just recently, that for some strange reason kept wanting to spend time with me, accept me the way I am and didn't try to change me. Them listening to me, me listening to them and experiencing parts of this life together played a big part in leading me to where I am now. After all, it was one of my best friends that literally told me, "You should write a book!"

I am also acknowledging my family. You enabled me the space physically and mentally to create what manifested in this book.

Martial Arts, the idea itself, manifested in the great trainers I was and am able to learn from, all the training partners that gave me the opportunity to grow and learn from each other are definitely worth a special acknowledgement.

Special thanks to my counsellor, too. You are a beast at listening, and I couldn't be more thankful that I found you at what seemed to be just the right time.

Not to forget every single person I met so far, no matter how briefly, to serve as a mirror that showed me a little bit more of what I am or at least of what I trick myself into thinking I am.

Thanks to Savvy Book Marketing for helping me bringing this book into a grammatically correct form that makes it easier to read for everyone.

Lastly, I feel the importance to mention THC and psilocybin. Two molecules that never failed me at changing my state of consciousness and so enabled me to look at things from a different angle.

About The Author

Jonathan Rohrer was born in 1992, and grew up in a small village in the south-west of Germany. He was brought up in a very strict Christian family. When he realised that neither the Christian teachings nor the bible itself were giving him answers to the questions he had, he started going on a search, a search that every human being is probably more or less on. One to find meaning or just for the answer to the question: "What is it all about?"

That journey led him to different places, and he looked and listened everywhere but couldn't find anything until he ended up living in the northern jungle of Thailand for a year. There he learnt to let go and open himself up, which led to a lot of realisations and the first notes, which revealed themselves to be the foundation of this first book, without him even knowing at that time.

Introduction

Why am I writing this book? I am not going to deny that I feel something you could label as pride towards the realisations put down in this book. And it will give me something you could label as joy if many will read and enjoy it. But in the first place, whenever I have a good idea or read something that seems very smart or wise to me, I feel the urge to share that – to be a guide, or rather a little signpost on other peoples' journey. I want to show what I found out to present a new perspective and new ideas. That doesn't mean that they are right or wrong. I don't want people to say, "He is right," or "He speaks the truth." All I wish for you is to keep an open mind and allow yourself to look at things from the perspectives I describe in this book. And if it doesn't resonate with you at all, that is totally fine. Bruce Lee put it very wisely in his philosophy of Jeet Kun Do: "Absorb what is useful, reject what is useless, add what is essentially your own."

I spent pretty much exactly one year, from October 2019 to October 2020, in the jungle of northern Thailand – in a village with the name of Pai. During that time, I learned a lot. I practised Muay Thai in the local gym. I met a lot of different people. Some of them very briefly, some became dear friends. I was surrounded by nature. I smoked a lot of weed and experienced psychoactive mushrooms a few times.

I read some good books. I started listening to some good podcasts where an actual conversation happens. And I started online therapy. With all that and constantly great weather for the first time in my life, I experienced months without a depressive episode. Some of my bad habits got better. I developed a confidence I never had before.

At some point, I started writing down notes. It started just as a plain Text-Document on my laptop. I named it 'Realisations'. Every time something came to my mind or I read or heard something that seemed wise to me, I wrote it down in this document with a number in front. By the end, the count was at 21.

When I went back to Germany after that year, I was sure that with what I learned, I would continue to stay positive and share all this wisdom with my friends there. I would reconnect with my family. Everything would be different than before I left. And in the beginning, it worked. I did run every day despite coming from tropical temperatures to the cold of the German autumn. I moved back in with my mother. And we had a conversation here and there that seemed to get us back together. But it didn't take long before old habits crawled in. I found myself trapped inside like everyone else because of the pandemic restrictions. And even though I did label myself a loner – until I dropped giving labels entirely – I started missing and craving social interaction. So the depressive episodes came back. I went back to hiding in my room and avoiding my mother and everybody else living in the house as best as I could.

On Christmas 2020, a dear friend I met in Thailand sent me a card, writing that she read a book that was transforming her. So, I bought that book and started reading it. It was called "Awareness" by Anthony de Mello. As I was in a bad place mentally at that time, it really spoke to me. This book didn't seem to try to sell me anything. The author didn't seem to have any intention of convincing me of his opinions or beliefs. At the same time, he was writing on topics that have been weighing on my soul for my whole life. With this book, he gave me a way of looking at things from a new perspective, and many of those angles of looking at life made a lot more sense to me than what I had believed so far. But most importantly, he recommended an exercise for the reader: To watch oneself without judging.

He wrote that for some people, it takes years until that exercise results in any change or understanding of oneself. For me personally, it took one day until I started writing down things I realised about myself I never thought of or identified with before. And over the following days, these realisations started to change the way I was looking at life. It was a very drastic change from a fundamentally nihilistic view to a more welcoming perspective towards the future.

Just as I was on that new high by the wisdom this book shone on me, I went to visit a friend I hadn't seen in at least one and a half years. And since she didn't participate in the social media game, we didn't really have any contact during that time at all. We had a lot of catching up to do and had a great time talking and sharing what we had learned in the time apart. In the evening, I took my laptop and opened that Text-Document backup for the first time since writing down the last entry. And as I read it out loud to my friend, I became more and more shocked at these words I myself had written down. I thought most of it is probably just gibberish I had thought to be smart when I was high on weed. But not only did I still see these notes as very smart and helpful or even wise. Some of them said pretty much what I had just read in that book, Awareness, months after I saw those notes for the last time. That book about truly living.

My friend was also amazed by these notes and told me I "had to write a book." So I started doing exactly that. Trusting that some people will read it just at the right time in their lives, so they are open to these words and find in themselves what I found.

As I was going through my notes, I felt like some of them don't really belong in that book, and others were so similar that I merged them into one chapter. Furthermore, I added some more chapters because I still continue to have more realisations. So, in the following 16 chapters, I tried to put my thoughts about those realisations into words that are supposed to reach as many seeking minds as possible.

I want to leave you to enjoy reading this book with two quotes by Alan Watts:

"It is hard indeed to notice anything for which the languages available to us have no description."

"Words can be communicative only between those who share similar experiences."

Chapter 1: Balance

There is balance in everything. For example, there is a balance between males and females in every species. Some fish even have mechanisms to readjust that balance. They can switch their gender. So, if there aren't enough specimens of one gender for the natural reproduction process, they can simply adjust.

There is a balance between plants and animals. They need each other and kill each other at the same time, which is no contradiction. Some organisms are turning oxygen into carbon dioxide while others are doing it the other way around, and there always has to be a balance between the two. One could say, "But the balance can be off. Right now we are looking at a higher CO_2 concentration in the atmosphere since records began. And it has devastating effects on all life on our planet." That is true. There needs to be a certain balance of those two gases in the atmosphere for most living creatures on earth right now to survive. But a different balance will be the perfect environment for other beings to thrive. So it is really just a matter of perspective where this balance actually lies. But we will discover more about the matter of perspective later in this book.

We all know that we need a balance in our diet to be healthy. If we eat too much or too one-sided, we get sick and sluggish. But if we don't eat enough, it's exactly the same.

Our body needs to move and it needs to rest. Every organ in your body has its function to keep the balance between certain substances.

One last example that made it very clear to me. We need to consume water in whatever way. Our body consists largely of it. You can die of it, too, though. Not only by drowning. There are reports of people who died from something you could call water poisoning. What is basically happening is that the balance of water and electrolytes in your body is off, which is causing your brain cells to swell and ultimately prevent the blood flow, which again can lead to death. I don't want to scare you, it takes about 5 litres of water consumed in one hour for an adult to go fatal. But what this is showing is that even water, the most fundamental substance for every living being on earth, can be a poison if not consumed in balance with other nutrients.

There is another thing that needs balance, and this one is hard to get our heads around. Especially with a western upbringing. Chaos and order. We are indoctrinated by our parents, governments and religions that we need as much order as possible. A structured life, where we can't get surprised by anything. Get a safe job with a good salary so you never have to worry about money. Keep your room in order so you will find whatever you need when you are in a hurry. It's no surprise that a disorderly room can cause unnecessary delays. We don't want these delays since the appointments or tasks assigned to our days demand us to be punctual.

Of course this makes sense to us because if there were no order at all, so pure chaos, nothing would get done. There would be no language, because even language is some kind of order with its rules. If I wouldn't follow those rules, you couldn't understand what I am writing in this book. There would be no food to eat and no houses to live in.

Even the most primitive (or at least what we call primitive) civilisations have some order. There are jobs for everyone to do. Some hunt, some gather, some take care of the children and so on. But the magic word here is 'some'. Of course we need some order. But we also need some chaos. Unfortunately, the word chaos brings forth negative associations in our western brains. When we think of chaos, we picture riots, burning buildings and people smashing in each other's heads. That's a possibility of total chaos in the modern world. But again, I am talking about the balance between chaos and order. So while this would be the one extreme, the other extreme is probably best described in the book 1984 by George Orwell. A System where everything is overlooked and every hour of the day is strictly appointed to a certain activity.

The gender of every newborn child is chaos. The structure of a growing tree is chaos, as is the dancing of a flame or the falling of a leaf. Imagine all these things would be ordered, structured. You would know everything about a child before it is born. All the trees would look exactly the same. As would every flame and every leaf. And everything else. Life would be 100% predictable. Doesn't that sound very boring?

There must be a balance between order and chaos. If you try to order everything in your life, you will ultimately fail because chaos will arise. It always does. The more you live in order, though, the worse the chaos will hit you. And you will have a much harder time dealing with it.

Furthermore, the more order you are trying to attain, the more chaos you will create with it. Because again, there is always a balance. It occurs naturally. We just live in the illusion that if we just try hard enough, everything will become ordered. If you look at the societies with the strongest laws, the strongest police force, you see that they also have the most crime. When we order our food supplies with monocultures, we create great chaos in the natural food chain. Then, because we drive out certain animals from the place used for growing food, others will multiply and in turn, eat the food that we wanted to grow for ourselves. Those are mostly insects. So, we introduce animals in the area again that eat those insects, but those in turn thrive on the big food supply and become a plague themselves. Then we use chemicals instead, but that turns out to be very unhealthy for us, and it gets into the drinking water. So, you see, the more we try to order things, the more chaos will arise, and we are not better and not worse off than we were before.

I conclude, therefore, that it is wise to have balance in everything. For this last example: Order the most necessary and welcome the chaos with curiosity, because aren't the unexpected things in life the most interesting, the ones that bring the most joy?

Chapter 2: About Judgment

My original note on that was: "People are judging us, and that's okay. We are doing it too. We should just always be open to let this person prove to us that our judgment was wrong."

It is true that we are judging each other, and we are judging ourselves. And we are imagining others judging us. And we are imagining others thinking that we are judging them. If you are confused now, that's okay. It can get complicated, but we can break it down. Let's look at what judgment fundamentally is.

You are looking at an action or event and evaluating if it is good or bad. That's basically it. Let's say you look at a person dealing with their child and you are thinking, "It is wrong to treat your kid like that," or you might even jump to the conclusion and think, "This person is a bad parent." You could exchange the words "wrong" with "right" and "bad" with "good", and it would be exactly the same. Now you feel good about the action this person has done, but you are still judging them. You are evaluating what is done.

The question is: What do you base your judgment on? On moral, you will probably say. Well, that leads to some more questions. What are your morals based on? The experiences you have had in your life so far. By what are those experiences influenced? Your parents, your culture, your religion and the people around you, who themselves are influenced by the same institutions.

So, in the end, it is not really you judging, but the role you are playing, created by these experiences and influences. You might say, "Well, this is who I am. The experiences I made formed my present self." At this point, I have an exercise for you. The next time a judgment comes up in you, turn your attention towards it. Ask yourself, "Where is this coming from? Which influence is responsible for me judging this?" You will be surprised how much that will show you about yourself. And you will not only understand yourself better but also be more aware of where the judgment from other people is coming from and learn how to deal with it in a more calm and understanding way.

Chapter 3: Growing (Up)

For me, like for most children, the idea of growing up was not desirable at all. It seemed boring and stressful at the same time. What I really wanted was the freedom of deciding to do whatever I wanted to, but what I wanted to do was not what most adults did at all. Sooner than I thought, I got more and more freedom, but at the same time, the responsibilities grew. And I had decisions to make I didn't feel ready for. This might sound familiar to you.

My response was to avoid any responsibilities and simply never grow up. Be Peter Pan. It worked quite well. I just never saw myself as a grown-up. Never stopped playing and learning. It brought in me a great deal of depression though, because I thought that I am supposed to grow up at some point, and I was afraid of that. At some point though, I realised that that is life. Playing and learning. I realised too that I was fighting the idea of growing up because I was afraid of it. As soon as we lose that fear, growing brings great joy.

We often trick ourselves into a role. "I am a teacher, so I know what and how children need to learn," or "I am a carpenter, so I know how to make furniture." And we are so scared of not living up to this role, of not being seen as a grown-up. We come to forget that in the end, we are all students of life. Teachers can, if they are open to it, always learn from their students. I myself don't have children, but people who do have their own are saying quite often that they learn from their children about things they never thought about before. And I think that is because children are not preoccupied with the influences we have been living with for decades. They don't hold back and when they get curious about something, they just ask or try to figure it out. So, they are asking questions we might be too afraid or too ashamed to ask.

There is a term I came across a lot recently and I like it way better than 'growing up. It's simply 'growing'. This doesn't imply an end to it. No magical number. Like 16 or 18 or 21 or 25 years old. "Being better than yesterday" would be another way to put it. Or a very scientific approach I remember Elon Musk saying was something like: "Every day, aspire to be less wrong than yesterday." And the important word here is *aspire*. Because that won't happen every day. You might even feel like you are taking steps back. But if you don't even try to get better, you never will. This is saying two things for me.

First: There is nothing wrong with not knowing something and asking about it. It is very freeing to start asking questions or saying, "I didn't understand that." Not only does that give you the chance to actually understand it, because the other person will most likely try to make it clear to you. But they will also notice that you are actually listening and not only pretending. And they will realise that the way they are explaining or talking about something might not be the best for others to understand. That way, they are getting valuable feedback. So, both of you are learning something. Both are teachers and students at the same time.

Second: Everything I believe at the moment might be wrong. That might be a hard pill to swallow. Especially if you identify with being smart or with having much knowledge. You will see that it is very freeing to not see your current understanding of the world and yourself as *the truth*. You can act accordingly to what you think you know at this moment. And if that perception changes in the future, you can say, "I was wrong back then. I know better now." And if you will be able to use the exercise from the last chapter and not judge yourself, especially not for something your past self did, you will never have to grow up. You will keep growing by default. You will not only learn but also be able to let beliefs and opinions go. A great way Joe Rogan likes to put it is, "I am not married to my ideas." Meaning if you are confronted with a new viewpoint on something, it is totally okay to change your opinion on it. There is nothing to be ashamed of.

What seems to be the biggest problem for us in changing our opinion on anything is that we think that makes us switch sides. "I was on the wrong team the whole time?" one tends to think.

Well, in western society, we are raised with binary thinking. Religious or scientific, good or bad, right or wrong, teacher or student, healthy or unhealthy, and so on. But as we just saw, you are always teacher and student at the same time. And as we have seen earlier, things can be healthy and poisonous at the same time, depending on the dose. So is water good or bad? Again, we need it to survive. We need to drink, wash and clean. But water in the form of a flood can also be very destructive. While for the lobster in the restaurant kitchen, it can be the way to escape its fate as dinner and survive for a little longer. That means everything is on a spectrum or can be seen from different perspectives, just like colours.

Most of the time, when two factions are fighting about who is right, the answer is somewhere in between. It's like two people fighting over the colour of a car. One is saying it is green while the other is sure it is yellow. As we know, there aren't just six or eight colours. There is an infinite spectrum of them. We just named a few. And there is a colour that is somewhere on the spectrum between green and yellow. So, if the car appears to be coloured exactly like that, neither of them is right, and they are both right.

"According to the CIA Factbook, the length of the UK coastline is around 12,429 km or 7,723 miles. According to the **World Resources Institute**, the length is around 19,717 km."

This sentence is taken straight from Wikipedia. Some of you might think, "How can these two measurements result in such a big difference?" The rest has heard of the term "coastline paradox" before. On first thought, it shouldn't be too hard to get an exact measurement of a coastline with modern technology. But a coastline isn't straight. It has curves and ripples. The closer you zoom in on a map, the more of them appear. Meaning what was one clean radius at a certain scale becomes a radius with many smaller ripples on it, which makes it way longer if straightened. If you keep zooming in on a satellite picture, at some point, even the edge of the water isn't a straight line. But you see the wavy line that the water leaves on beaches. You could keep doing that until you reach an atomic level and beyond, if technically possible, and resultantly, the length of the coastline would increase infinitely. So there is no right answer to the question, "How long is the coastline of the UK?"

While these are just examples, all answers we come up with are just a one-sided view. If we accept that, we will stop fighting over opinions, just as we stop fighting for opinions of 'our team'. Because there are no teams. We make them up. Just as we make up sports teams. They wear shirts that display a city name, and we are cheering for them and arguing about whose team is better or who deserves to win a tournament, although it doesn't have any impact on our personal lives. It just does because others around us picked the same or a different team. So we can be happy together or feel superior to others. But in the end, the whole game is made up.

As soon as you say, "I don't care who wins anymore." your emotions are not tied to the outcome of games anymore. So, in the same way, you can stop identifying as politically left or right, conservative or liberal, young or old, living this side of the mountain or the other. And as you do so, you are not tied anymore to the opinions of the team you thought you were in. That makes you free to think and say whatever you want. And you are not tied to that, too. Then you can say, without any regret: "I was wrong back then. I know better now."

So you don't have to stop at one point in your life and say, "This is my standpoint, this is my team. I'm gonna align all my life choices with it." You can keep growing, like a tree, every day a little bit. Until the very last day.

Chapter 4: Freedom

It seems like the best word to me to describe what we are all looking for: Freedom. The illusion that drives us to chase careers rather than doing things that truly make us happy is often given the name of financial freedom. The idea is to not have to worry about money because you have enough of it or enough coming in every month. But that is rather financial security than freedom. And there is no ultimate security. No matter how much money you have, there can always be a financial crisis that makes it worthless. You can be robbed. Not by people in black overalls and masks that come into your home at night. But lawsuits, for example, can drain you financially. And the more money you have, the more responsibilities. You have to entrust it to a bank or, even better, invest it. Which again means you have to worry about the investments. So, while you are free to choose where to live and what to eat and buy whatever you want, there is constant worry and mistrust. In that way, instead of giving you freedom, the money is actually enslaving you.

Some people see freedom as not being restricted by a government with laws and rules. So they try to overturn it – a revolution. You could argue that former revolutions made things better for the people at the time. But in the end, a new leadership replaced the old one and made new rules that looked quite similar to the old ones. Because whenever people live together, there has to be an agreement to at least a few rules. Otherwise, they try to take advantage of each other. As I wrote in the first chapter: If there is too much order, chaos will arise and vice versa. So there will always be a balance.

What these ideas of freedom are trying to do is solve an internal problem with external solutions. You see, the enslavement – which you could look at as the opposite of freedom – doesn't come from outside but from within yourself. This might sound like a very abstract idea but let me try to make it clear to you. There are two things that enslave us. Fear and desire.

Let's start with the one that's easier to understand. At least in my view.

The one fear that unites us all is the fear of death. It seems to be unbearable to us to not know what happens after our body dies. So we turn towards religions. Often we get raised with one and so are brought up with one of those easy answers and follow through with it. We enslave ourselves to the rules given by this religion. So we give up our freedom for a cure for that fear of death. But it doesn't really cure it. It rather gives us hope. The hope that our religion, our 'team', is right. And so, if we live according to the rules of it, we hope to go to whatever place is promised. And I have a few words to say about hope in a later chapter.

The fear of not being seen as a valid part of society or

whatever community is most important to you makes you wear certain clothes and have certain hairstyles. So you give up the freedom of choosing your appearance. It even makes you afraid of changing your opinions, as we have seen earlier.

When it comes to desires, it gets harder for us to understand or accept why they should enslave us. Aren't the things we desire to do giving us freedom? Like our favourite sport, dancing, making music, playing games, or just working on whatever we are interested in? Well, when we engage in those activities, we enter a state of consciousness we call the flow state. It's when all your attention is focused on that one thing you are doing. During that time you forget all of your problems. You might even forget about the physical pain you used to feel. And you lose track of time. It's what children have when they are playing. All of that sounds very desirable, right? But what happens to the playing children? At some point, a parent is calling them because it's dinnertime or bedtime or time to go home. Just as any game or dance or music session or any other activity has to end at some point, we get drawn back into reality. And with it, all the worries return. The ticking clock reminding us that we are getting older and will die at some point. The dispute we have with someone. The worries about the economy, finances, security.

There are people who perfect doing just that one thing

that brings them to their flow state. You may have seen the phrase 'wake up, '[fill in activity]', eat, sleep, repeat' on a shirt. It works to a certain extent. For a big portion of their time, these people are happy. They are in their flow state. But whenever they can't do this thing for whatever reason, they fall into a deep depression. They feel worthless, like nothing makes sense anymore. Isn't it interesting that the people we see as the most successful often fall into the deepest depressions, drug addictions and even kill themselves? It is exactly that. When they are on stage, in front of the camera or on the football field, they play their favourite game. They are on their high. But every mountain has two sides. If we climb it, we inevitably have to get down the other side. And the higher the mountain, the deeper the valley behind it.

We all are doing exactly the same, just on a lower level. So we often don't fall that deep. But after a great experience, there is always that feeling that something is missing in our life afterwards and we are longing for that feeling again.

There is a great analogy I like to think about. Our life is like a free fall. The moment we are born, it is already clear we are going to die at some point. So we are, metaphorically, pushed down the cliff, and we know we will hit the ground. You might remember the first time you realised that you are going to die. It feels like the cartoon character that runs over the edge of a cliff. The first few seconds, he keeps running in the air, and it seems like everything is still alright even though his fate is sealed already. But the moment he looks down, fear takes over. Now your childhood is over and real life begins. After the first shock, you realise it's quite a long fall. So you relax for the moment. But then you see people hitting the ground, and they are just seeing it at the last moment. But you also see other things falling. Things to hold on to. Even big patches of ground, some with big trees on them. So you go to the nearest tree and hug it tight. And as long as you close your eyes and feel that tree and the grass under your feet, you forget that you are falling.

Those trees are our desires. Things, places, tastes, feelings and people. We cling to them as hard as we can. Because they give us the illusion of safety. Just like health insurance. But things break, places change, meals get dull, feelings fade, and people let you down and die eventually, just as you do. No matter how good your health insurance is, it won't save you from death. It just postpones it.

So, does that mean we should hide in a hole so we can't get hurt by losing those things? Or even turn to suicide to make an end to this anxious existence? Well, of course not. There is nothing wrong with enjoying the company of the people you love or a great meal. Or whatever brings us joy. But we don't have to cling to it. As soon as we are saying, "I can't be happy without XYZ," we have lost. We have lost our freedom to a desire.

So going back to the metaphor of the free fall. Enjoy the

fall. Only that will give you true freedom. You can visit those places, but as hard as you try to hold them, eventually, they will disappear in thin air. So, always be prepared for that. And if you find yourself free-falling with nothing to hold on to, maybe you will remember one of my favourite phrases:

"There is nothing to do and nowhere to go."

Chapter 5: Don't Workout Because You Hate Yourself

Workout because you love yourself. Because you deserve to have a healthy body.

A friend recently messaged me saying she started working out because people said she is too skinny. After a short time of exercising daily and looking at herself in the mirror, she realised that she doesn't find herself too skinny at all. She felt good just the way she was. More importantly, upon having worked out, she felt all the other benefits of training the body. She felt stronger and more energetic.

Funnily enough, I have gone through pretty much the same process. I though needed years to realise that there is nothing wrong with my body. The societal standards influenced my view on how a male body should look like. I am still grateful I started working out and have kept doing it for many years now. The physical and mental benefits are just too great.

This is why challenging your body physically is, in my opinion, always a good idea. What I see happen a lot though and what I experienced myself is that we often make a negative feeling the foundation for our exercise rationale. We start by feeling too big, too skinny, too lazy.

Don't get me wrong, I am not attacking your inspiration. Whatever gets you involved with physical training in whatever form and capacity is great as long as it gets you started. But wouldn't it be great if you would do it driven by positive emotions, like knowing your muscles will get stronger, your posture will improve or it will be easier for you to move? Rather, we start by thinking, "I need to do this to lose weight," or "I need to look more like this person." Such a premise indicates a sense of dissatisfaction with yourself. Thus, dissonance takes place within.

This is not supposed to be a chapter to make you motivated to work out. Maybe your job is physically challenging enough so you don't need any additional workout. I intend to use this way of positive thinking and translate it into all areas of life. Such as seeking someone else's company to avoid feeling lonely rather than wanting to enjoy spending time with the person. Or listening to music not because you cannot endure the silence but because you love the sound of music.

As we have learned in the last chapter, our desires enslave us. Meaning if we desire a certain type of body, we will always have that suppressing thought of "I should work out more." If we desire spending time with a certain person, we will always have that suppressing thought of "I hope this person has time for me." Such enslavement is not good for the soul. At the end of the day, it will brood anxiety, insecurity, or other negative emotions within.

I think it is great to do things you love and try to better yourself in a way you feel able to. It should neither come from fear nor desire, though. But only because it feels right to do it and it will be fruitful for you in some way.

Chapter 6: People Change

Western academia has held this notion for a very long time. It's that the human identity is formed during the first five years. If you are quiet at the age of 5, you will be quiet and introverted for the rest of your life. The same goes for narcissism or any other personality labels we invented over time. While this is a very simplified description, I believe that there are still many people who think that way. How often do we tell ourselves, "Well, this is just the way I am," or "I can't help it."

I recently had a conversation with a friend. She said she met with someone we used to hang out with in our teens. Their lives went in different directions, and they didn't see each other for years. After talking for a little bit, my friend felt like she didn't know that person. I think she said something like, "Was she always that basic?"

My thought was that while my friend grew quite a lot in those years – and as we have seen earlier, that entails letting go of a lot of things too – the other person did not seem to have changed too much.

I tend to think that we change all the time. In a way, life is change. Most cells in our body get renewed completely within 7 to 15 years. So if you meet someone again after 15 years, there is not much left of the biomass from the last time you saw them. In the same way, your brain makes new connections in every moment of your life. But as we saw in the last chapter, we like to cling to things. We cling to opinions and world views and to a personality we project on ourselves. "I am a Christian," "I am an artist," "I am a gamer." Saying those things makes us feel like we belong somewhere, and everything that doesn't add up to our construct of identity can't be true. So anytime something comes up that doesn't fit our current belief system, we don't want to hear it. We get angry. We even fight it.

At such a place, it is a great exercise to ask yourself why you get angry. You will see that it is always because a belief of yours is getting challenged. And that makes you defensive of your current belief, which you see as part of your identity.

Sometimes though, convincing evidence comes regarding your outlook being out of place. You take action and change quite dramatically.

There is a great story I like to tell. It's the true story of Daryl Davis. Daryl is a black R&B and blues musician living in the USA. One day he played at a club like many times before. After the show, he talked to one of the last visitors who stayed at the bar for a while longer. After talking for a while, the guy told him that he is a member of the Klu Klux Klan or KKK. The KKK is one of the most racist groups in modern society.

Daryl didn't get mad but kept talking to him, and after a while, the guy said, "I've always been told that blacks are all evil. That they are robbers and murderers and rapists. You are the first black guy I have a conversation with and you seem to be alright."

They exchanged numbers and promised to meet again. They did, and after a few meetings of just talking as friends, this guy realised that Daryl was just another human like himself and that he couldn't go on following an organisation that did not accept him as a member of society. So he quit the KKK.

This was a big step because he surely left behind not only ideas but friends, a community, a place where he felt safe and strong and accepted. To this day, more than 200 people have left the KKK because of Daryl Davis. Daryl admits he didn't convert or change anybody. He just showed them how ridiculous their beliefs were patiently. He did so not with arguments but by honestly expressing himself, by being himself. He showed them that he is just like them. A human being, with a family, problems, worries, hobbies and everything else that connects us all.

There are two things to learn from this story. First: people change. But everybody can only change him- or herself. So you are the only one who can change yourself. Other people can prod or inspire you but in the end you are always the one who makes the decisions.

Second: while you cannot change other people – and how often would we love to just do exactly that – you can help them and point them in a direction. Not with words or specific actions. But by expressing yourself honestly. And again, that is what Daryl did. He didn't try to show that man how wrong he was. He just wanted to hang out with him because he saw that he was more than the racist the man showed everybody and himself to be, hiding behind an organisation that made him feel like he belongs to something. He saw a human being with problems and fears and joys and a family just like himself.

With everything you do, you inspire people just as you get inspired by others. Think about the power that gives each one of us. Not by trying to force anything into place. But simply by choosing to express ourselves honestly and not lying to ourselves by showing what we want to be rather than what we are.

Chapter 7: The Outside

After diving deep into philosophical questions and maybe being overwhelmed with abstract thoughts, I wanted to take a step back and write about something relaxing and not so hard to grasp. The outside. Outside your room, outside your house, outside the city.

In our day of age, we say things like, "I like the outside," or "I like outdoor sports." If we think about it, that used to be the norm. Our ancestors used to live most of their life under the open sky. They only spent time inside houses or tents or whatever they built to sleep and cook and shelter from the force of nature.

It wasn't long ago when we started shifting our workplaces, living spaces, playgrounds and pretty much everything inside houses. Many of us lost connection to what we know as nature. The world outside with hills and trees and flowers and wild animals. The smell of fresh air and the warmth of the sun.

You can put down this book for now. Take all the questions you have in your mind with you outside and take a walk, it can be very refreshing. You might even want to make it a part of your routine.

Chapter 8: There Is No Right Decision

After our little timeout, let's go back to the philosophical ideas that make our western minds itch. There is a lot of talk about the question of free will. Do we have it? Is it a hoax, an illusion? To put it differently, are we making decisions for ourselves or is something else making them for us? The more popular theory is that we are just following a foretold path, our destiny, God's path or whatever you want to call it.

I like to look at it from a different perspective. We always make decisions. Every second. Even if we lay in bed and do nothing, we are deciding not to get up and do some activity. That much should be clear.

As it goes, the bigger the decision is that we have to make, the more we wonder afterwards if it was the right one. We might even say to ourselves that it was probably a mistake.

Let's look at how decisions work and what makes us decide if something is a success or a failure.

We can agree that every decision is followed by an outcome. Based on our goals and values, we label that outcome as either good or bad or as success or failure. But we will never know where the other outcome would have led us. We can also evaluate those decisions and estimate based on similar decisions we or others have made in the past. At the end of the day though, it's just guesswork. The only way to know where our decision would have led would be to turn back time and try the other option, or rather multiple options.

Even then, one of the paths we could have taken might have a better or worse outcome way ahead in the future. So to truly know which decision would be the best, we would have to live every option until the end to see which one is the best. And even then, we just looked at it from the perspective of our own life and not from that of our children for example. We will never know for sure, it's just speculation.

If you try this experiment with your imagination though, living out many possible outcomes for all possible decisions, you will probably come to a point where you start asking yourself, "Which one is the best outcome now really? What do I truly want in this life?" And when we are really honest with ourselves, we know that we don't know what the best possible outcome is. That is why we pick teams like religions, political parties, etc. Such associations give us some kind of rule book and expectations for what our life should look like. But if we let go of the idea that we belong to any group, there is no expectation left to go for.

So we can conclude that there is no right decision, just the one you made. Or, to put it differently: There are no mistakes. That feels wonderful to read, doesn't it?

Let's take it on a visual level. We all know those drawings that visualise our life as a path. Often it is a person standing on a splitting path leading in two directions to two different goals. I don't like those illustrations because they imply that there is one decision you make in one direction, and then you just follow that.

As I just said, we make decisions all the time. They just pop up out of nowhere. It's like the path has hills you don't see behind or sharp bends with bushes. And after them, BOOM, the next decision. It is splitting all the time. And once you have taken one option, all the other ones disappear.

We will never know where they would have led.

And it doesn't matter.

Because they are not part of the reality that has transpired.

Chapter 9: Don't Ever Think You Are Too Broken To Be Fixed

The Japanese art "Kintsugi" (golden joinery) describes fixing pottery with silver, gold or platinum. I find that a beautiful metaphor for life. Because it is a way to not only fix things but make them subjectively even more beautiful than they have been before. So, when you find a good way to fix yourself, think of it as gluing yourself back together with gold. So the more you are broken, the more you will shine in the once broken places. As Rumi also said, "Wound is where the light enters you." You can proudly show the light to everybody.

Most things I am describing in this book, you may have to experience it to really understand. There are many things we can't describe with words because language is just a tool. And like any other tool, there are situations where they work very well and others where they are not very practical.

Take, for example, the old problem of describing colours. Try to find words to describe any colour to someone who is blind from birth. It's impossible. In the same way, how can you describe the idea of relief from pain to someone who has been in pain as long as they can think or, on the other hand, never experienced real pain?

For many years, I knew that it is not good for myself and the people around me when I fall into a mental state where I can't cope with some thoughts. That's where I'd be overthinking the meaninglessness of my existence and the existence of life in general. Every once in a while, I'd think about talking to a therapist. But every time I came to the conclusion that there is nothing another person could say that would change my mind. And in a certain way, I was right. Because as I know now, I am the only one who can change my mind. And that is true for everybody.

I eventually got in contact with a counsellor though. I don't want to get into terminology here, but I don't mean a psychotherapist when I say a counsellor. It was not someone who tries to understand your problems then finds solutions for you. But someone who helps you to understand yourself or rather your former self, the personality we identify ourselves too often with and that way gently picking up these pieces and moulding them together with gold. Over time I realised more and more that there is, in fact, nothing wrong with me. That there is nothing to fix but the way I am thinking. The way I am reviewing my own experiences.

Just as there are many different materials one can use to fix pottery thinking.s and moulding them together with gold. Over time I realised more and more that there isnderstexperiences that make you feel miserable. One of them surely is a counsellor. Someone you only talk to in a professional context so you can trust him or her to not tell anyone else about your deepest fears and desires. And also someone who knows how to gently push your thoughts in directions that show you more about yourself. It's not so much about what you are telling this person but what you hear yourself saying aloud. And the thoughts and feelings that are coming with that. Even though you might think you thought about this one issue so many times and always came to the same conclusion, you can realise so much more.

In the same way, you can talk to a friend or a family member. Someone you trust. That can have the same effect. But often we are embarrassed about some feelings, so we might not want to talk about everything. Whatever we feel comfortable with is definitely worth sharing though.

I also did many things I thought that I was embarrassed about because I thought I am weird for doing it. But once I talked to one or several people about it, and they told me that they also think about or do the same thing, it made the anxiety and embarrassment go away.

Another great technique to try is writing things down. It doesn't have to be a journal or any other structured way. Just take a pen and anything to write on and start writing. Don't worry about grammar or any other technical aspect. Just write down what's in your head as well as you can. If you want to make sure that nobody will ever read it, you can destroy the paper immediately. Or you can keep it and read it later. Just as you sometimes struggle to find words when talking to somebody, you will probably find yourself in the same situation here. But again, that's okay. It's more about the thoughts and feelings you experience while writing than what you are actually putting on paper.

If you like drawing, try that too. But don't force yourself to draw exactly what you picture in your mind. Just draw whatever you feel like. And don't judge yourself based on your skills. The purpose here is catharsis and self-comprehension.

Whatever way you will try to approach understanding yourself better, it can be very helpful to take some time afterwards and relax. Maybe have some tea or coffee or whatever drink or snack you like. Go for a walk or just sit or lay down and watch yourself. Obviously, I don't mean in a physical sense like looking into a mirror. But just watch yourself as if you were someone else. Get curious and ask yourself as if you are a third person, "What is he doing? How does her body feel like? What is he thinking about? Which emotions are coming up in her?"

Try doing all of that without judgement. Whether positive nor negative. No judgements at all. You might be surprised by what you find.

Chapter 10: Don't Be Afraid To Ask For Help

I touched on this topic earlier when writing about growing (up). We already saw that if you ask for knowledge, not only do you learn something, but you give the other person the opportunity to learn something too.

Now, sometimes we want to ask for other things. Like, if we can borrow an item or if somebody can help us move. The usual. We might hesitate because we don't want to bother the other person or feel like we are asking too much or can't give enough back. And then there is this saying, "It's more blessed to give than receive."

I have been not asking for help many times because of exactly these reasons. But I made some very interesting discoveries about asking for help. The first one is: People love to help or rather to feel needed and useful.

Two things we humans strive for is attention and recognition. If you watch children, this is all they do whenever they are not playing. They are trying to get attention with whatever they do. And when they feel like they achieved something – and be it just jumping down from that little wall ttention and recognition. If you watch children, this is all they do whenever they are not playing. Thwant to show it to others. We want them to see us and we want them to recognise our creation.

Therefore, just by asking someone to help you or to show you how something is done, you give them attention. You signal that you want them to be part of your circle, that they matter to you. So, even if the person declines for whatever reason, he or she will feel recognised and knows that you trust him or her with that task. They often might not show that, but it is almost always true.

The second discovery I reached: When we feel uncomfortable asking the same person too often for help, it is mostly because we want to keep up an image of being humble. I think that being humble is a great virtue. But like any other trait, it is often more important to us that we are seen by others in a certain way than to actually live like that. So it can be more humbling to say, "I don't know how to do this, can you show me?" or, "I can't do this alone can you help me with it?" than "I can figure doing this on my own. I don't need to bother anyone."

Lastly, I want to talk about the "giving has a higher standard than receiving" idea. In a certain way, it comes down to the same thing I just wrote. The "I want to be seen as a nice giving person and not the one who is always asking and never giving." Well, here we are being thrown back all the way to the first chapter of this book: Balance.

There is always a balance between giving and receiving, too. If you like to give help, you don't have to be shy to ask You will find people will be more willing to help becau' they know you as a generous person. It is not a counting game though where you put the good deeds you did on one side of the scale and ask for as much help until the scale is even. Just help whenever you can and ask whenever you need to.

When I was living in Thailand, I was astounded by how the locals I made friends with shared everything. I realised after some time that our western understanding of sharing differs very much from what they are doing. When they accept you as a friend or in fact if only one of them brings you along and says, "This is my new friend," they will share almost anything with you. Even as a stranger, I was receiving way more than I was ever used to. They are very aware of that cultural difference because they are working mostly with tourists and travellers. So, they are not pressing you to do the same. They would in return show a lot of respect and gratitude if you do rather share, though.

After watching them for some time, I even realised that they don't even ask each other. If I need a scooter to go to the store and mine is not available at the moment, I just take one of a friend. I can always take a cigarette if the pack is lying on the table because whenever someone asks for one, I will give my last one away. This implies a lot of trust with each other inside the community, and no doubt there are people taking advantage of that. But I personally like that way of living way more than doubting each other all the time just because there is a person every once in a while that takes advantage of generosity.

So giving isn't automatically better than receiving. In fact, you could see them as equal. In that way, you never have to feel bad to ask and in return, don't have to see yourself as a saint for giving. Both can be just a part of life.

Chapter 11: Never Forget The Value Of Time

There is a great song from the cartoon show "Adventure Time." It's called "Time Adventure." Yes, the song name is the show title, just the two words are switched, but that's not what I wanted to get to.

The first line in that song goes, "Time is an illusion that helps things make sense," and it follows with "So we're always living in the present tense." I like that as an explanation of the term 'time' a lot.

From a philosophical standpoint, there actually is no time. There is just the present that we are experience right now. The future is just predictions we make. So it is a thought, a construct, made up by us and therefore, it is just an illusion. Just as the past is only memories in our minds that are quite flexible. And even though we can record things with different media nowadays, nobody ever knows what exactly was in the past. So this too is just an imagination in our thoughts and therefore, an illusion. That was a lot of philosophy in a few sentences, but again this is not what this chapter is about.

I am pretty sure that every language has a word for time, and we are using it all the time to be able to communicate ideas. That's what I am going to do in this chapter too.

Try to think of something that happened in your life that

made you feel very bad. Like a breakup, getting fired from a job or losing someone important. Remember how you felt immediately after. Maybe you actually experienced something similar not long ago and still feel that way. If you can relate, then this chapter is especially for you.

When something like that happens, we all cope differently. Some of us take it with us for a very long time. If we go back to the metaphor of falling from a cliff, we'll see that we have been hugging one of those trees very tight, and without warning, it has disappeared. Most of the time, we can't believe it's gone. We were holding it so tight just a second ago, and now it's gone. That's very hard to accept.

In the first moment and maybe even days and weeks after, we tell ourselves we can never be happy again. We feel like we can handle some change, but not that much. My favourite tree, gone forever. After some time goes by then, we accept that nothing can be done about what is gone. Even if it continues to hurt sometimes, we remember that I AM STILL FALLING! So we find another tree. That also takes time.

If you lose a job, you will eventually find another one. After a few years working there, you might even forget how dramatic it was when you lost your previous job. It's just one of many life events that brought you to where you are right now. If you lost someone dear, the feeling might come back from time to time. But most likely, it won't be as bad as it was immediately after the loss. So even after the worst incidents in our lives, after a few years, we go from feeling horribly bad to feeling sometimes bad or even not really having any emotion tied to the experience anymore. So, don't forget the value of time. It can be very healing.

We often forget the value of time when learning something. In most cases, the problem is that the learning curve is very steep in the beginning and slowly flattens as we get better at a skill. That is a crucial time period where we are easily discouraged because we see others that are at the high end of the skill level. We feel like we are making no progress at all while we actually do make progress. It may just be very little with every training session. But very little progress every day over a long period adds up to a lot of progress. It sounds very obvious, but we often lose focus or think we are just not good enough or lack the talent to get there.

There is a very easy way to show yourself that you do make progress even if you don't feel like you do. All you need to do is compare where you are right now to where you were some time ago. That time frame can be, for example, one month. If you practice whatever you do every day, you will see a difference already. Maybe not a big one but some. It will show you at least that you are not stagnating. And then afterwards, compare what you did one month ago with where you are one year later. Boy, oh boy, you might be surprised.

If you are trying your hand at drawing, you can mark progress easily by just storing your drawings and trying to replicate the work or draw something similar in the same style again. If you are trying athletics or racing for instance, measure your time and write it down. If you are practising playing an instrument or a sport, make a video for before and after purposes. If you make a video of yourself playing one song or doing one combination and then make a video after one year or half a year of regular practice, you will see a change. It is just important to compare yourself with your former self and not with anybody else.

Chapter 12: The Truth Is: There Is No Truth

In our modern western society, we have this idea that with science, we can disprove the supernatural ideas presented by religion and or supernatural elements such as ghosts or any other kind of inexplicable magic. Everything we can measure and prove with experiments or rather are unable to disprove is seen as a fact.

The example is, the earth circles the sun. That seems to be true. But if we make a more exact measurement, we see that the movement doesn't describe a perfect circle but is slightly elliptical. So, if you just want to make clear that the earth is going around the sun and not the other way around, almost everybody would agree with you if you say, "The earth is circling the sun" when in fact, it rather ellipses the sun.

Well, if you thought I am done here, that was just the start. Our moon is also not just circling the earth, but earth and moon are circling their common centre of gravity. From the sun's perspective, the earth wobbles on an elliptical path around the sun. The important word here is perspective. We could go on and take into account the movement of the sun itself in perspective to the galaxy it is inhabiting, the Milky Way. Or rather the black hole in the middle. And then the Milky Way in perspective to other galaxies. So, it really depends on what you take as a point of reference.

If we go back to just looking at the earth and the sun, we are just saying that we are going around the sun because all the other planets do so. That's because it is the heaviest object in the solar system. And if we make a model, it seems very obvious that the sun is in the middle and all the planets are circling it. But if we take away all other objects, there is no way to say if the earth is going around the sun or the other way around. If we see the sun as the reference point, the earth is going around it. But if we see the earth as the static reference point, it is the sun going around. And since there is not one point in space we could declare as the reference for everything, it is all the same.

Let's look at some examples easier to grasp. What is down at the North Pole is up at the South Pole. North is not up. We just decided at some point to draw all the maps that way. I guess we did so because on a compass, the needle is always pointing north, and it probably seemed logical that on a map, it should point upwards or away from us. But it could also point towards the reader of the map or downwards. Then all the maps would look upside down to what we are used to. But there would be nothing wrong with that. They could still be used just as well as the ones we have now. It's again just a matter of perspective.

If you are standing on the bottom of the numeral 6, you would say it is a six. But when you are standing on the opposite side, you would say it is a nine. If you look at a cylinder from one side, you will see a perfect disc. While from another perspective, it is a rectangular surface. And when you move around it, it will appear in many different shapes. Your brain is just telling you it is a cylinder because you have seen and touched one before, so it is rendering this two-dimensional picture into a three-dimensional shape that you already know.

One last example now because it really blew my mind, and I love to think about it. Maybe it will give you some joy, too. When we are talking about objects, we are saying they "are" a certain colour. "This flower is red." Isaac Newton discovered that the sunlight seems to be white but also contains all the colours of the rainbow – the colours that are invisible to the human eye. So, objects actually are absorbing all the colours except the one we are seeing. So you could as well say, "This flower is everything but red." But that is just linguistic gymnastics. What's really interesting is that if you shine the flower with monochromatic light, for example, yellow, it will appear to be yellow. In fact, everything illuminated only by monochromatic yellow light appears to be yellow. Because this type of light does only contain yellow. So, every object illuminated by it can only reflect yellow, of course in different shades though, otherwise you wouldn't be able to make out any objects.

You can actually do this experiment with just a computer

screen. If you darken a room as much as possible and put a white picture on the screen, you will see everything in that room illuminated in the colours you are used to. If you change the picture to another colour, you will see how everything will look like this one colour, just in different shapes. In that sense, the flower is red in perspective to sunlight or white light. At the same time, it is yellow in perspective to monochromatic yellow light.

So, we can conclude that there is no "one truth," but only truth in perspective. Once we realise that and really take it to heart, it makes it easier to accept that people believe in different truths. And it makes us more open-minded to other perspectives because we can accept it as just that, another perspective, instead of trying to figure out who is right or wrong.

Chapter 13: People Hurt People Because They Got Hurt

The better-known saying is probably "Hurt people hurt people."

In the Thai Boxing Gym I am training at, we are sparring regularly. That means we are putting on protection on the shins, thick gloves and mouth guards, to train for fights. The goal is that nobody gets hurt while both fighters can use their techniques as freely as possible. To get the most out of it, we are changing partners after every round. So, I would sometimes spar way better opponents and other times with people not as experienced as I am.

When I was on the lower end, I would sometimes get hit a lot while I hardly managed to land any strike or kick. Again this is just training, so it doesn't really hurt. But it still is hurting the ego. And because I wouldn't be able to get him or her back, I let it out on the next opponent, who would be less experienced.

This is one great thing about martial arts. You learn a lot about yourself. And that was just one lesson for me. When I get frustrated with one person because I don't have the power to get revenge, I take it out on someone else. And that someone a lot of times is me.

I think this is a very common pattern recurring in most humans. We can see it often in parents passing problems on to their kids. They maybe get bullied by their coworkers or even their boss. Since they don't have the power to fight back, they bring that aggression and longing for revenge back home. Maybe not even consciously. But something is nagging in the back of their mind. And then the kid gives them the slightest reason by making noise or disobeying an order. Now they have someone to put it out on. Not necessarily physically, but maybe just with words. The child in return feels bullied or treated unfairly, but because he or she is powerless, again, they take it with them to school or to their siblings. This is just a very common example, but this characteristic can affect any chain of human interactions.

While we always hope or wish to stop that chain by changing the people that hurt us, the only way is to look at ourselves and become aware of where we mistreat others. I am, after all, the only one who can change myself. And that applies to everybody. The evil boss, too. So no matter how much wishful thinking and action we use to try to change the other person, it won't help. It can be very frustrating to try and accept this, but the sooner we do, the better for ourselves and everybody around us.

An exercise that helps me understand my own behaviour is watching myself whenever I get angry, frustrated or aggressive. In most of those moments, we tell ourselves that the other person is wrong and we are right, which justifies whatever intense reaction we create. Screaming, getting violent or maybe just feeling those emotions arise and keeping them inside. Everybody is dealing differently with frustration, but that is always the starting point: Frustration.

Alan Watts wrote that the often-cited Buddhist phrase, "Life is suffering," might be better translated as "Life is frustration." So to bring it back to fear and desires: we get frustrated because of the desire to change that unpleasant environment or because of the fear of being unable to do so. Put it any way you want.

This leaves us again with watching ourselves very closely whenever this feeling of frustration arises, when we feel our blood boil and are tempted to harm others or ourselves.

Additionally – and I know this is particularly hard ed to harm others or ourselves.is feeling of frustration arises, wheg unable to do so. Put it any way you want.ng, getting vyourself if that person is actually having a problem with you or if they have just been hurt by someone or something else.

After all, the only way to bring change is to be aware of yourself and the world around you.

Chapter 14: You Don't Need To Hope

Hoping is just worrying while doing nothing. Or rather wishing for a certain outcome of a situation. Or the other way around: it is being afraid of a certain outcome.

So there it is again. The desire and fear. Let's look at another imaginary story.

Say you visit a local animal farm with your young daughter. You observe many different animals. Chickens, goats, cows and even two donkeys. The child is amazed and loves watching all these different creatures. In the following days, she keeps talking about the animals and asking if you can go back to the farm.

One day you say, "We won't go to the farm, but we will go to another place. I'm sure you will love it." She is disappointed because she is imagining seeing the animals again that she liked watching. She was really hoping you would go there again.

What you didn't tell her though is that you are on the way to the zoo for the first time. So, after a long car ride of disappointment, because she is not getting what she was hoping for, this young human reaches the zoo and sees before her eyes all the exotic animals she has seen only in pictures or videos. For the first time, they are moving right in front of her eyes, live. After thinking the donkeys and cows are big, she is filled with awe looking at a giraffe. It seems immeasurably tall. Of course, this is way better than the farm.

What I am trying to say is that when we indulge in the act of hoping, we are wishing for an imaginative outcome either to happen or not to happen. But that imaginary outcome is always based on our experience, on the past, which is not even existent. It is just our memories of the past. In fact, it is impossible for us to imagine something new. Because how can we know how interesting the zoo is going to be when we have never been there?

Now, of course you can turn that around. Maybe you don't want to go to the farm again because it was boring. You know all the animals already. You have been there countless times and would much rather go to the zoo again with all the really interesting animals. But for some reason, your parent makes you come along on a trip to the farm. So again, there is a disappointing car ride full of hopes to be somewhere else. This time you are trotting behind, not really looking at the animals. All of a sudden, you become witness to the donkey giving birth. Again it is something you are seeing for the first time, and you are amazed and puzzled about the scene of a baby animal coming out of an adult one. This is way more interesting than the zoo.

I know these are cute stories about a child learning about the world. You might indulge in hopes about way more serious things. Something like your company's success, like getting to keep your prestigious job, or that this lump you are feeling is no cancer. But that implies that you know that your life with that great job you really enjoy doing or a life without cancer is better than the alternative. But you don't know it, as we have seen in the chapter, "There Is No Right Decision."

I came across quite some people that got impacted by great tragedy, either to their own health, or the health or life of their loved ones. And looking back at it after a certain time, they realised that this horrible event led their life on a path that turned out to be great.

There is one example I really like. The American rapper, known as Action Bronson, used to be a cook before his rap career. He really enjoyed cooking and still does. But he was always interested in rapping, too. He just never found time or motivation to really pursue that path as more than a hobby. One day he slipped into the kitchen and broke his leg. So now, at least for a period of time, he couldn't work in the kitchen anymore. I don't know what his thoughts were, but we can speculate they went something like, "I wish this never happened" or "I hope this is not keeping me from cooking for too long."

As he couldn't cook anyway and wasn't able to move much, he concentrated on writing songs and recording his first album. It was a hit and the start of a successful – in terms of wealth and popularity – rap career. Furthermore, because of this wealth he gained, he started doing cooking shows and got recognised more than he might have ever imagined for both his rapping and cooking.

We can very well assume that he never hoped to break his leg. But that event turned out to be hugely beneficial for his career.

When I was younger, after fighting for a long time about it with my parents, I got to have a cat. He was from a shelter and just a few months old. So I took him home and raised him. I loved him very much and he seemed to enjoy spending time with me too. But he was reckless. Several times he would sneak into some neighbours or our own garage without anybody noticing. So he would get locked in at night. And of course every time I would get worried and be very happy when he would turn up the next day after someone opened the garage in the morning. He would be very hungry and complaining.

One morning, he didn't come home. He must have been three years old. I was hoping he was trapped somewhere again and that he would turn up the next day. But he didn't show up the next day either. After looking for him everywhere for a few days, we found out that he had been run over by a car.

Of course, that was very hard for me to register at the time, and writing about it now still brings a little tear to my eyes. But not long after, I decided to go on my first travel.

An adventure that gave me the opportunity to get so many new impressions and perspectives by visiting other countries and discovering other cultures. I would never have left my cat at home to do that. So if he hadn't died that young but lived until old age – which I definitely hoped for at that time – I would have stayed in Germany for probably another ten years or so. And who knows where I would have been now, given those turn of events. I would probably not have been writing about the importance of perspective, fear and desire and the uselessness of hoping.

I am very grateful for all the experiences I was able to have, the people I met, realisations I had and fears and desires I was able to let go of because of travelling. Of course, I would still love to sit here with that little animal on my shoulder. I shared so much with him. But that scenario was not for me to decide.

This recollection actually makes me think of my favourite scene in the movie, "The Lord of the Rings: The Fellowship of the Ring." It's when Frodo says to Gandalf: "I wish the ring had never come to me. I wish none of this had happened." And the Wizard responds: "So do all who live to see such times, but it is not for them to decide. All we have to decide is what to do with the time given to us."

While I am writing this book, the world is in the midst of a pandemic that has greatly affected most peoples' life. Most see it as a very negative event. And sometimes I hear sentences like, "I just hope everything goes back to how things were, soon." But the farm has been destroyed in a storm. It has to be rebuilt. Do you really want it to be rebuilt exactly the same as it was before? At least some improvements would be nice, wouldn't they? Or maybe a whole new concept could make it even better.

Life is change, and change is life. The less you are fighting it, the easier it gets.

Chapter 15: Stop Trying To Fix Things

I believe that one of the fundamental sources of suffering is that we see the world in terms of problems and solutions. When I see situations like Native Americans trying to defend their land from an oil pipeline that supposedly pollute their water, I ask myself: When did we humans take a wrong turn? When did we start to exploit the earth and each other? And more importantly, why and how?

I do have a theory now.

It probably all started when our ancestors stopped hunting and gathering and became settlers. Why did they do that? Was there not enough to hunt anymore? I don't think so. My theory is that someone started to see hunger, cold, predators and eventually death too as a problem. It may seem obvious that those things are problems. But we have been socialised for thousands of years to see the world in terms of problems and solutions.

So, we see people suffering from hunger and sickness and thirst, and we are trying to help. But let's get back to these people a few thousand years ago, building the first houses and fields and having livestock. They did – according to my theory – see those 'problems', and as they started looking at it that way, they were looking for solutions. Because this is the way of the world, if you have a problem, you need a solution. Otherwise, it's not a problem. If you are hungry but you say to yourself, "It's okay. I'm gonna find something to eat eventually," it's not an immediate problem. And you are not looking for a solution.

But if you do see it as a problem, you are looking for solutions. And so, our ancestors started planting things and keeping alive animals in fenced areas. They built better shelters that eventually turned into houses. And so they solved the problem of hunger (at least as long as natural forces did not destroy their fields), cold, fear of wild animals. But now they had to deal with a whole lot of newer problems. For example, they had to get rid of weeds in the fields so their plants could grow better. Or they would have to protect their livestock from predators. Then they would find out that if one grows the same plant in a field for several years, the field gets drained of nutrients. So, they had to come up with a system to organise the fields. As the fields got bigger and the work harder to do, they invented more and more tools. And now they were at a point where they had to devise all these different kinds of labour. People were specialising. Soon every village had a smith, a horse breeder, a butcher, a tailor, a lot of farmers and so on. Now, they had the problem of how to distribute work and goods in a fair way. And as people started to fight over who is entitled to what, they needed someone to govern the community. Someone who makes laws and makes sure that everybody respects the law. Because after all, only that is fair, right? But what to do with the people that don't abide by the law?

I could go on and on, but I think you get the point. Today, we have so many and so complex problems that nobody could ever solve them. Just look at how many laws we have. There is even a professional whose only job is to figure out which law fits a problem that went to court: Lawyers.

We also see how big of an impact our way of living has had on the earth for the last one hundred years. We have polluted the air by burning fossil fuels, the water with plastic and radioactive waste, the earth with chemicals and monoculture. We have cleared most of the forests and meadows and driven out or made extinct so many animal species.

So as you can observe, we are desperately trying to fix everything. But I have a secret for you: No matter how hard we try, we may fix one problem, but we will create ten new ones. Even if we put a bunch of mirrors in space to reflect the sunlight and the earth stops heating up again, we will create a whole new spectrum of problems. In the end, we still have this enormous growing population of humans on earth. We solved so many problems. Everything becomes more and more "secure." Health standards rise and rise. We become older and older. But we have to die in the end anyway.

Don't get me wrong, I am not a pessimist. I understand the urge to help people who don't have enough to eat or access to clean water or live in other horrible conditions. But that won't solve the problems in these places in the long run. And if you are looking into why poverty exists and what could be done about it, you will realise that it gets infinitely complicated. In trying to solve one issue, you will create new ones. It's an endless ironic cycle. Just look at the countries in the east that the USA "liberated" from their dictators. They got rid of one problem. But how many more did they create?

Let me tell you about a small people in Tanzania. The Hadza. They are the last hunter-gatherer tribe in Tanzania. As the resources they need become less and less, they are slowly forced to join the modern world. There are people supporting them, and there is video footage of them getting interviewed. It is very interesting to listen to what they say about western society. They have never been to America, but they have been visited by westerners, and so they know about our way of life. They laugh at the ideas of houses and doors. They are puzzled over why people are killing each other and themselves, how we are putting elders in a centre and letting strangers take care of them. Or why we have toilets. And while they are talking about all these serious topics, they are laughing, laughing wholeheartedly because they don't understand the use of all that.

At the same time, they have an extremely high child death rate. At least compared to the 'civilised' western countries. They have no hospitals if someone gets injured or sick. They don't have churches, priests, judges, politicians, teachers, movie makers, airports, bottles, sinks, cars. Why? Because they don't see inconveniences as problems.

If they don't find anything to hunt one day, they simply don't eat or make do with just whatever they gathered. No need to accumulate animals in a farm because they are afraid of not finding something tomorrow. If someone gets sick and dies, he just dies. That's what happens to all living things.

Just when we start to see a problem as an inconvenience, we start looking for solutions, and as we can see all over the world and throughout history, these "solutions" only create more problems.

We can see exactly the same thing in our own personal life. When we see not having a secure job as a problem, we are searching for a solution. And thankfully, there is a job market providing just that for you. Now that you are sitting in front of a desk all day you have the problem that your body gets lazy and unhealthy. So you squeeze a one hour workout in your already small amount of free time. Now you have even lesser time for your family. So you try to make it up with weekend trips and vacations. But that's expensive, so you need to work harder to make more money. This continues until one day you are burned out.

That is just an example, and of course, I don't wish for anyone to live like that. But it is one of many prominent patterns that can be observed in numerous lives within our civilised, modern world. And what is it all for?

It's no wonder we are like this. All because we have been raised that way. And sadly, we are doing it to our children too. You are not performing good in school? That's a problem, let's get someone to help you. You are not eating enough, too slow, not at the right time? You have to do it that way, because that is the right way. Other kids are laughing at you? That's a problem. I'm gonna talk to their parents. That way, we are raised to care about everything. How we look like, what time we eat, which words to use, what to be scared of.

What if we would stop over-concerning ourselves with the way we look, how we talk, not having the job, our car, or the life we want? What if we would stop seeing those things as a problem? There wouldn't be the need to find a solution. And therefore, there will be no need to fix anything.

You could argue that this is cowardice. That in this way, you leave all those people suffering while we live this comfortable life, exploiting so many other humans. But you have to remember that you are one human in a worldwide system that involves billions of people. Of course, you can make a change. You can avoid certain products. You can donate to certain causes. You can even go to work for an organisation that helps people in more desperate circumstances.

But you have to ask yourself: When do I allow myself to be at peace? When nobody is dying of hunger anymore?

When you saved 100 people from dying of disease? When there are no more homeless people in your country? When there is no animal mistreated anymore? Or do you just do whatever feels right to you and allow yourself to be at peace without everything being the way you would wish for it to be?

So, you don't need to try to fix things, but you also don't need to try not to fix things.

Chapter 16: Be Kind

The impression we get from around us a lot is: Being nice doesn't get you anywhere. If you want a promotion, you make your colleagues look bad so that you stick out as the best in the pool. If you want to be popular in school, you bully weaker kids. If you want to make money, for example as a salesman, you talk people into buying things you know they don't really need.

When you're a man, being kind is often seen as a weakness. It makes you vulnerable and others might make fun of you. I feel like this is deeply rooted in our capitalistic society. Ideas like "only the strongest survives" are popularised. And again, being kind is often seen as a weakness. So we are kind to our loved ones, the people close to us. But the further away somebody is emotionally from us, the more we distrust them.

"He could have bad intentions, so I'd rather take advantage of him before he does of me." That happens to be another recurring thought pattern.

At the same time, we are trained to always do better. So not only are we not kind to others, but we are also not kind to ourselves. We are left with questioning ourselves, "Could I've done better? Am I working hard enough?" And when we fail in our own perception, we beat ourselves up about it. Some might argue this is healthy for self-improvement. But

I think this is one of the core problems of our society.

How many conflicts arise because of one person thinking he or she is not living up to something? And that something is always imprinted on that person's mind by someone else. Their parents, peers or society. Hurt people hurt people. I've been writing about it before. And sometimes we are being hurt or rather are hurting ourselves because we can't live up to an idea. An idea such as working hard enough, the idea of looking good enough, the idea of being masculine/feminine enough or the idea of having a successful career or earning a certain amount of money. Of course, this list could go on for a long time, but I think most of us can find at least one example we can identify with.

I didn't really plan this, but it all comes back together in this last chapter. I've been writing about how we judge others and ourselves, and it is exactly because of those ideas (Chapter 2). Just as being grown up is one of those ideas (Chapter 3). The fear of not living up to them or the desire to do so are enslaving us (Chapter 4). Just as they are the ideas that make us do things out of hate for ourselves instead of love (Chapter 5). And just because we don't live up to the ideas imprinted on us, we accuse others of being the same and therefore are left with judging them instead of starting a dialogue with open minds to learn from each other, like Daryl Davis does (Chapter 6).

Sadly, we are often too ashamed of those feelings we all

share, just in slightly different ways so that we don't open up and allow ourselves to heal and find peace of mind (Chapter 9). These ideas sometimes make us so embarrassed or proud that we won't ask for help; we become so stubborn that we rather try to do it all alone (Chapter 10). It is those ideas that make us try to get to the goal as fast as possible, and that makes us forget the value of time (Chapter 11). They are keeping us narrow-minded and with that, keeping us from accepting other perspectives (Chapter 12). It is also those ideas that make us unnecessarily hope to have or become something in the future instead of being thankful for what we have now (Chapter 14). Just as they make us hurt ourselves and others because we feel like we don't live up to them (Chapter 13). And it is those ideas that make us trying to fix things, that don't need any fixing after all (Chapter 15). Last of all, they prevent us from being kind; not only to others but also to ourselves.

I want to make clear at this point that I am not against having ideas. It is just as fine to have and like them as it is to have friends, to enjoy your food, to do whatever makes you happy. But don't tie yourself to them. Always be aware that whatever you do or have is only for the moment. And you have to be able to let go of it in the next one.

I am convinced that first identifying these ideas and then letting go of clinging to them will automatically make you become kinder to yourself. Because there is nothing to live up to anymore. You realise that you are enough, just like the way you are, despite anyone telling you anything different. And in turn, that makes you be kinder to others. Because nobody can hurt you anymore. So everybody wins.

A great exercise is seeing yourself as a child – not grown up yet but still growing. Telling yourself, "It's okay to make mistakes. I am still learning." And I mean it when I say that this applies to every age.

Lastly, I wanted to remind you of the exercise that helped me a lot and still does. Being aware. Watching oneself as if you were someone else. And very important: Without judging.

Never mistake kindness for weakness!

Epilogue

This book is an attempt to put the realisations I had in my life so far into written language. That might have worked out well, more or less. The fact that you have been reading it until here though, at least shows that I caught your interest, and that makes me happy. I made you think. Maybe just a little bit, maybe quite a lot. Maybe you agree with most of it and maybe you are strongly disagreeing and don't like what you have been reading at all. Either way, I planted a seed and in some of you, that seed might grow and that way, my words could be a hint, little helpers to help find what was in you the whole time. A finger pointing to the moon.

There was one thing that I had to learn many times in my life and that is that it is *my* journey and no one else's. There have been people who thought they knew where I have to go. I had been following their ideas because I thought they must know where to go. But I had to realise that everybody, including me, has to find their own way. Other people's thoughts put into words – spoken or in writing – can always just be a sign, a pointing, a little hint. But you have to go the way yourself.

Seek, and you will find. I am sure that it is true. You might find something very different from what you were seeking in the first place. But you will find.

On the following page, I want to list some books and

movies/shows that have been helping me a great deal on my journey. But it is not only in books, movies and podcasts that you can find wisdom. If you look and listen closely, you can see and hear it everywhere.

"If the eye is unobstructed, it results in sight; if the ear is unobstructed, the result is hearing; if the nose is unobstructed, the result is a sense of smell; if the mouth is unobstructed, the result is a sense of taste; if the mind is unobstructed, the result is wisdom."

- Unknown Author

Books

Awareness: Conversations with the Masters by Anthony de Mello

The Way of Zen by Alan W. Watts

Siddharta by Hermann Hesse

Personality Isn't Permanent by Benjamin P. Hardy

Tao Te Ching by Lao Tzu

Freedom from the Known by J. Krishnamurti

Movies and Series

The Truman Show

Jim & Andy: The Great Beyond

The Midnight Gospel

The Fountain

www.ingramcontent.com/pod-product-compliance
Lightning Source LLC
Chambersburg PA
CBHW050045120526
44588CB00038B/2747